MW01008070

Why Are You Here
and Not Somewhere Else

Selected Essays

HARRY L. DAVIS

Harry L Davis is the Roger L. and Rachel M. Goetz Distinguished Service
Professor of Creative Management at The University of Chicago Booth
School of Business.

The University of Chicago Press, Chicago 60637
The University of Chicago Press, Ltd., London
© 2013 by The University of Chicago
All rights reserved. Published 2013.
Printed in the United States of America

22 21 20 19 18 17 16 15 14   2 3 4 5

ISBN-13: 978-0-226-11113-1 (cloth)
ISBN-13: 978-0-226-11662-4 (e-book)
DOI: 10.7208/chicago/9780226116624.001.0001

Davis, Harry L.
 [Essays. Selections.]
 Why are you here and not somewhere else : selected essays / Harry L.
Davis.
     pages cm
 ISBN 978-0-226-11113-1 (cloth : alk. paper) — ISBN 978-0-226-11662-4
(e-book) 1. Business education. 2. Management—Study and teaching. I.
Title.
 HD30.4.D384 2013
 650.071--dc23

                                        2013025543

WHY ARE YOU HERE AND NOT SOMEWHERE ELSE

CONTENTS

Rethinking Management Education: A View from Chicago with Robin M. Hogarth

Introduction

Uncertainty has always played a major role in business. And in recent years managers have had to grapple with an additional source of uncertainty: the challenge to redesign—even reinvent—their organizations and businesses on a continuous basis. The pace of change has accelerated. We live in an increasingly interdependent world. Product development times and life cycles are shorter. There is greater diversity

This article is an edited version of Selected Paper Number 72, originally published in 1992 by the Booth School of Business. Without implying endorsement of the ideas expressed in this paper, we wish to thank the following for comments on a previous draft: F. R. Heath, Stephen J. Hoch, Steve Lorch, Albert Madansky, Harry V. Roberts, and Bill Whitney. This essay was made possible by a grant from the Albert P. Weisman Endowment. Robin M. Hogarth is professor emeritus at Universitat Pompeu Fabra in Barcelona, Spain. He was formerly the Wallace W. Booth Professor of Behavioral Science at the University of Chicago's Booth School of Business and also deputy dean for full-time MBA programs from 1993 to 1998.

in the workplace. Few firms can cling to fixed beliefs about products, markets, and operating procedures and expect to succeed.

This onrush of change has forced management to rethink assumptions about how to organize employees. Of particular importance are issues of breaking down functional silos and the flattening of organizational structures. Among factors fueling this trend are the need to react swiftly to changes in the market, to incorporate quality in products and services, and to utilize fully the expertise of those employees closest to customers and products.

Given these trends, many firms face a key strategic question: How to develop and nurture managerial talent capable of thriving in the new environment?

Here, we consider the role business schools can play in helping firms meet these challenges. In doing so, our major focus is on MBA education, although many of our comments also apply to various forms of executive education. While MBA education has blossomed over the past forty years, it is in danger of becoming irrelevant unless it can respond to the evolving needs of the business community. In partnership with firms, business schools should offer the education and self-development opportunities managers need. But to do this requires understanding the components of effective managerial performance.

MBA Education in the New Millennium

Since its inception at the beginning of the twentieth century, MBA education has gone through distinct phases. Many of today's most prestigious institutions were created between 1900 and 1955. Yet during this initial period they remained a relatively unimportant source of managers for U.S. corporations.

Between 1955 and 1960, the business community challenged business schools to "get serious." The schools responded by upgrading the faculty and other resources and succeeded in becoming first-class institutions. A significant component of this coming of age was a closer alignment of MBA curricula with traditional university values.

During the next twenty-five years, MBA education boomed. The annual number of graduates nationwide exploded, going from about 5,000 to 70,000. Business schools became important suppliers of managerial talent to U.S. firms, and despite large fluctuations in economic and business conditions, the schools flourished.[1] Today, MBA degrees adorn the walls of many office suites at top U.S. corporations.

Starting around 1985, business leaders and students challenged schools to make MBA programs more relevant to their needs. Businesses require a broad range of skills and effectiveness from the people they hire. Students also want more. MBA candidates today are older than their earlier-counterparts, and the real-world work experience they bring to the classroom makes them impatient with the academic concerns of their teachers.

Today we stand on the threshold of a fifth phase in the development of MBA education. Schools have two options. They can continue to do business as usual and risk growing irrelevance. Alternatively, they can reevaluate their mission and operations and devise educational agendas that have significant added value for both students and businesses.

Components of Effective Performance

In evaluating our activities at Chicago, we have asked two questions: How can we enable our students to achieve exceptionally high levels of performance on a consistent basis? How can we add value to our students in a way that endures throughout their careers?

In our view, high performers are smart, savvy, and insightful. Smart means they have a lot of knowledge and know how to apply it. Being savvy means knowing what they want to achieve and how to do it. And insightful means they can learn and grow from their experiences. To explain the choice of these particular terms, consider the components of effective performance.

Effective performance is the result of actions. But what determines the quality of actions? Figure 1 provides a schematic representation of three important determinants of action in business settings, namely, conceptual knowledge, domain knowledge, and action skills.

FIGURE I. ELEMENTS OF PERFORMANCE

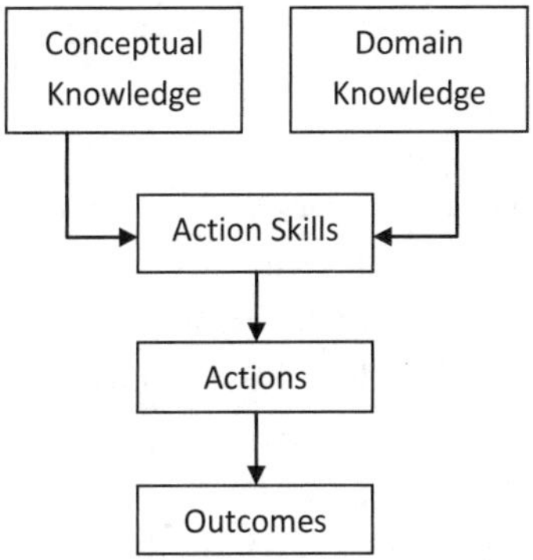

```
┌─────────────┐   ┌─────────────┐
│ Conceptual  │   │   Domain    │
│ Knowledge   │   │  Knowledge  │
└─────────────┘   └─────────────┘
        │                 │
        │  ┌───────────┐  │
        └─▶│Action Skills│◀─┘
           └───────────┘
                 │
                 ▼
           ┌───────────┐
           │  Actions  │
           └───────────┘
                 │
                 ▼
           ┌───────────┐
           │ Outcomes  │
           └───────────┘
```

Conceptual Knowledge

Conceptual knowledge is acquired through the formal instruction and learning experiences typically associated with educational institutions. It includes the formal education students receive in business school, such as training in economics, accounting, finance, statistics, marketing, organizational behavior, and so on. This body of transmitted wisdom constitutes the bulk of most MBA programs. It covers both pertinent business concepts and ways of thinking in a rigorous, logical fashion. The value of conceptual knowledge is that it develops the ability to think broadly and rigorously in business settings.

A solid foundation of conceptual knowledge is essential to effective performance and is acquired most effectively within educational institutions. Medical students, for example, do not have to rediscover through observation and experience how blood circulates. Where knowledge already exists, it makes eminent sense to use classroom instruction.

Even if the body of theory and concepts is incomplete, a solid grounding in conceptual knowledge has numerous advantages. In 1929, Alfred North Whitehead wrote: "The really useful training yields a comprehension of a few general principles with a thorough grounding in the way they apply to a variety of concrete details."[2]

Consider the economic concepts of sunk cost or discounted cash flow. A thorough grounding can prove invaluable if students are able to recognize situations in which the concepts are applicable in their subsequent careers.

In 1932, G. K. Chesterton argued even more strongly for the value of conceptual or theoretical training. He said, "The more serious is the trouble, the more probable it is that some knowledge of scientific theory will be required; and though the theorist will be called unpractical, he will probably be also indispensable."[3]

A thorough grounding in theory has long been a hallmark of the University of Chicago Booth School of Business and is much valued by both our alumni and the business community. In a 1956 paper titled "The Chicago Approach to Business Education," James H. Lorie articulated the rationale for providing theory within an educational institution. He justified this approach using the economic concept of comparative advantage:

> A university has its greatest comparative advantage in teaching underlying scientific knowledge and procedures; it has least advantage in trying to teach the detailed application of this knowledge . . . .
>
> We believe that this method of formal education best equips students to continue their education through experience once they have left the educational institution. They are better equipped to put their untidy and unpredictable experience into a meaningful framework; they are enabled to learn better from their reading and to know what to read; they are acquainted with sources of new knowledge; they are sensitized to important questions implicit in what they see and do during the course of their business careers.[4]

While we agree that universities enjoy considerable comparative advantage in teaching conceptual knowledge, we do not believe this is their only advantage. Business schools can—and should—go beyond the teaching of conceptual knowledge.

Domain Knowledge

Individuals acquire this knowledge by working at their jobs in particular firms and industries. It is pertinent to specific spheres of activity and may be acquired by experience or through formal firm or industry training programs. In addition, it can include knowing customers and suppliers of a particular business, a network of people in the work environment, a company's specific operating procedures, and an understanding of corporate culture. The key point is that domain knowledge is acquired through hands-on training and experience in particular job settings and is relevant to that domain.

Many studies have demonstrated that domain knowledge takes time to acquire and is not necessarily transferable to other areas.[5] It takes years of grueling practice to become a tournament-class tennis player, but this will not make one an outstanding golfer or squash player even though all three sports require considerable physical coordination. Similarly in business, expertise in finance does not necessarily mean success in sales; and effectiveness in, say, the trucking business does not guarantee effectiveness in banking. Domain knowledge does not transfer well from one sphere of activity to another.[6] Yet such area-specific, "practical" expertise is critical to performance. As stated by Roger Peters,

> You've got to know the territory. Jobs and Wozniak could not have created the Apple without expertise

gained through years of experience with small computers and other electronic devices. We become creative not by working on creativity as such but by mastering a domain.[7]

Business schools should not attempt to teach domain knowledge. There is no consensus on what specific domain knowledge should be covered; the acquisition of such expertise is a lengthy process, and employers are much better able to impart this knowledge according to their specific needs. On the other hand, business schools should teach students to respect the importance of domain knowledge in taking effective action. Moreover, they can impart skills that accelerate the ability to acquire appropriate domain knowledge.

Action Skills

Conceptual and domain knowledge are critical for high levels of performance, but they are not sufficient. Knowledge must be translated into action, and that requires action skills. These are the skills that enable individuals to set goals, to sell others on the value of those goals, and to work with and through others in their implementation. The value of action skills lies in the ability to achieve desired outcomes. Without action skills, conceptual and domain knowledge cannot lead to high levels of performance.

Where and how are action skills acquired? Most managers acquire them on the job, although business schools and firms often provide specific training in skills such as communication and presentation. To a large extent, it's a haphazard process. Yet there is no reason why the acquisition of action skills should be left to chance. Hard science can still be used to impart soft action skills. R. W. Revans's many writings on action learning programs make the argument that, in the arena of practical action, the scientific method is a powerful tool for business education.[8]

Effective performance is a function of conceptual knowledge, domain knowledge, and action skills. Colloquially, we describe managers with high levels of conceptual and domain knowledge as smart, and we describe them as savvy if they have good action skills. But that's not enough. Knowledge and skills need to evolve across time, and this depends heavily on how managers learn through experience.

Insight Skills

An old adage tells us that experience is a person's oldest and best teacher, and there's little doubt that we learn from experience. The questions are: What do we learn? And are the lessons of experience helpful or harmful to good performance?

To explore this issue, consider figure 2. This is an extension of figure 1 and emphasizes several points. Conceptual knowledge, domain knowledge, and action skills reside *within a person*. Actions take place *within a job setting*. In turn, the outcomes of actions affect the job setting in which they occur. This may be precisely the intent behind the action and is illustrated by the feedback loop linking the outcome back to the job setting on the left-hand side of figure 2. For example, imagine an action taken to handle a customer complaint that changes the customer's attitude toward the firm.

FIGURE 2. ELEMENTS OF PERFORMANCE

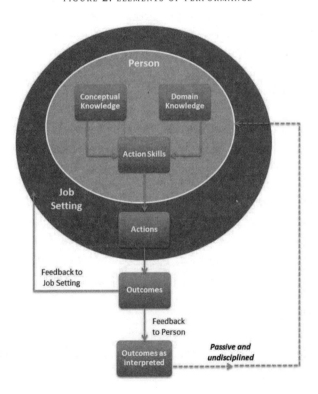

Finally, feedback not only affects the job setting but, as illustrated on the right-hand side of figure 2, has an impact on the person taking the action through his or her interpretation of the outcome. What then affects the interpretation of outcomes and how people learn from experience?

Many studies have demonstrated that people develop great facility in encoding or interpreting experience by simply associating actions with outcomes.[9] Moreover, for most tasks, this process occurs automatically in a passive and undisciplined way that requires little or no conscious effort. It is highly efficient behavior—people have learned how to learn.

Still, passive learning has its limits. It requires feedback that is timely, accurate, and relevant to the issues under consideration. Consider, for instance, the development of motor skills involved in learning to ride a bicycle. Here, feedback is both pertinent and immediate. Failure to correct an imbalance causes the rider to fall. Now imagine learning to ride a bicycle on a planet governed by different and unknown laws of gravity, where an imbalance does not necessarily lead immediately to falling. Instead, falling can be caused by an imbalance that occurred some time ago. In these circumstances, passive learning will not teach you how to ride a bicycle. In fact, your experience may teach you the wrong things.

There are many important situations where the interpretation of feedback is ambiguous and in which individuals have enormous difficulty learning the right lessons from experience.[10] If anything, feedback may reinforce erroneous beliefs, and even smart people fall into this trap.

To illustrate, consider the case of Benjamin Rush, a highly respected physician, professor at the first medical school in America, and one of the signatories of the Declaration of Independence. He advocated and practiced phlebotomy as a cure for febrile illnesses in the belief that the cause was excessive stimulation and excitement of the blood. When Rush fell ill with yellow fever, he prescribed plenty of bloodletting for himself. As reported by Eisenberg:

> From illness and treatment combined, he almost died; his convalescence was prolonged. That he did recover persuaded him that his methods were correct. Neither dedication so great that he risked his life to minister to others, nor willingness to treat himself as he treated others, nor yet the best education to be had in his day was sufficient to prevent Rush from committing grievous harm in the name of good. Convinced of the correctness of his theory of medicine and lacking a means for the systematic study of treatment outcome, he attributed each new instance of improvement to the efficacy of this treatment and each new death that occurred despite it to the severity of the disease.[11]

Though this incident is some two hundred years old and is taken from the field of medicine, it's not difficult to realize how comparable self-fulfilling and self-defeating actions can occur in business today. There are many situations where the choice of an action either prevents learning or reinforces existing beliefs without testing them. Consider decisions involving personnel selection (what happens to candidates who were not selected?) or certain types of investments and advertising expenditures.

As illustrated in figure 3, the interpretation of feedback in the form of outcomes needs to be an active and disciplined task governed by the rigorous rules of scientific inference. Beliefs must be actively challenged by seeking possible disconfirming evidence and asking whether alternative beliefs could not account for the facts.[12] These activities provide the foundation for insight skills and are the time-tested methods that were followed by people who gained some of the world's greatest insights, such as Bacon, Faraday, Pasteur, and Darwin. Indeed, when he compared the inferential methods of Spencer and Darwin, Will Durant made the following telling comment:

> Spencer began, like a scientist, with observation; he proceeded like a scientist, to make hypotheses; but then, unlike a scientist, he resorted not to experiment, nor to impartial observation, but to selective accumulation of favorable data. He had no nose at

all for "negative instances." Contrast the procedure of Darwin, who, when he came upon data unfavorable to his theory hastily made a note of them, knowing that they had a way of slipping out of the memory a little more readily than the welcome facts![13]

Darwin's insights have endured. But how many have heard of Spencer?

FIGURE 3. ELEMENTS OF PERFORMANCE

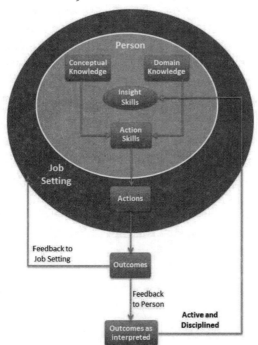

Our framework sheds light on the troublesome topic of intuition that is frequently discussed in business education, both favorably and unfavorably. Intuition is the result of learning from experience: people are not born with intuition! And the quality of intuition depends on how one extracts and interprets experiential data. In situations involving good feedback, it is easy to acquire good intuition. When feedback is ambiguous, the quality of intuition depends on the effectiveness of insight skills.

Our goal as educators is to help people become not only smart and savvy but, through the acquisition of insight skills, also insightful. Moreover, these characteristics are mutually reinforcing. Good insight skills accelerate the acquisition of both domain knowledge and action skills as well as the application and updating of conceptual knowledge.

Responsibility

To enable students to achieve exceptionally high levels of performance, the responsibility for learning should be shared between business schools, employers, and the students themselves. Many students are smart entering business school. And to make them smarter, business schools and employers should each teach what they teach best: conceptual knowledge in business schools and domain knowledge on the job.

Ultimate responsibility for learning action and insight

skills—to become savvy and insightful—rests with the students themselves. These skills cannot be acquired through study alone but require constant practice over many years in real-world situations. Students often are fascinated by inspirational accounts of others' successes. But "war stories" are rarely useful because the action and insight skills involved developed from each individual's unique set of talents and experiences. In addition, people must be motivated to keep practicing and improving their skills. Applying the concept of continuous improvement, the permanent honing of a person's action and insight skills should be seen as a precondition for consistently performing at exceptionally high levels.

While students should be responsible for acquiring and developing their own action and insight skills, neither business schools nor firms are absolved from responsibility in this process. On the contrary, both can play critical roles.

Business schools can provide students with a conceptual understanding of action and insight skills, their necessity, why they are difficult to acquire, and their relations both to each other and the two forms of knowledge. Students need a clear understanding of the components of effective managerial performance. Schools further need to provide students with opportunities for acquiring action and insight skills so that good habits are formed before they are tested in business itself.

Business schools can empower students to take responsibility for their own learning. Too often students behave like passive customers: they pay money and they receive an education. If the education doesn't seem to work, or they don't like it, then it's a bad product. In continuing education programs, the entertainment value provided by faculty plays a large role in reactions to courses. Without arguing against entertaining teaching, or against understanding the concerns and demands of students, we believe that if faculty pay too much attention to the superficial dimensions of student demands, they can unwittingly reinforce a passive customer attitude among students.

One implication of the comparative advantage argument Lorie used in "The Chicago Approach to Business Education" is that it would be wasteful for business schools to become involved in activities other than the teaching of conceptual knowledge. We agree that it would be wasteful for business schools to teach domain knowledge. Still, business schools have considerable comparative advantage over firms in getting students started on learning both action and insight skills, and these in turn greatly facilitate the acquisition of domain knowledge through business experience.

Business schools enjoy advantages in three areas that are critical to learning from experience: experimentation, feedback, and practice. Schools can function as laboratories in which students experiment and practice action and insight skills without downside risks to their careers. In addition, fellow students, faculty, and staff can provide frequent feedback, untainted by the personal or political factors within an organization. Finally, an educational setting provides time and opportunities that are difficult to find in a job, to practice different skills explicitly, to reflect on levels of achievement, and to spend time remedying deficiencies that would be difficult to examine in actual job settings.

These advantages and opportunities do not exist in all business schools. They must be created. Table 1 summarizes the arguments of this section.

TABLE I. ELEMENTS OF PERFORMANCE:
RESPONSIBILITY AND MEANS

	Elements	Responsibility	Means
Knowledge	Conceptual	Faculty	Study
	Domain	Firm	Work
Skills	Action	Students (but with help from faculty and firm)	Practice
	Insight	Students (but with help from faculty and firm)	Practice

Barriers to Acquiring Action and Insight Skills

It is difficult to learn from experience. In addition to the issues enumerated above, individual and social factors get in the way.

Smart individuals may have particular difficulty learning from experience.[14] This can pose particular challenges for the leading business schools, which tend to recruit smart students and then try to make them smarter.

Typically these students are considered smart because of their high capacity for learning from instruction, as measured by test scores, rather than their talent for learning from experience.[15] In fact, if their success in life to date is based on instructional learning, why should they invest in learning from experience?

Virtually all of these students' learning experiences have taken place in neatly structured environments, where instructors define the rules a priori. This is hardly good preparation for operating in more free-flowing environments where discovering the rules *is* the main task at hand.

MBA students, most of whom are still relatively young, are often given the benefit of the doubt if they fail. Such leeway dampens the motivation for self-examination. If anything, a youthful cockiness or a desire to protect their own positive self-images might lead these students to attribute their failures to other people or factors.

Learning action and insight skills is difficult and requires willingness on the part of the individual in at least four different areas: to question and alter one's beliefs in the light of new data, to recognize the importance of multiple viewpoints, to experiment, and to take risks and deal with the consequences of failure.

At the level of social interaction, learning from experience can be difficult because of the inherent risks of experimentation. Feedback, if offered at all ("If you can't say anything nice, don't say anything at all"), often is inadequate. Feedback in firms often comes in the form of annual or semiannual performance reviews, which in most cases is too little, too late. To be effective, feedback should be specific and closely follow day-to-day decisions and actions. For example, if someone fails to make a good presentation at a meeting, he or she should be told immediately—not six months later at a performance review. When feedback is not part of the organizational culture, seeking it can entail considerable downside risk for the individual.

Managers need to give and receive feedback. When this process occurs daily, the acquisition of action and insight skills can be considerably accelerated.

Further Implications

Our framework stresses the importance of having each component of managerial performance continually strengthen the others in a self-reinforcing cycle. For instance, practicing insight skills can improve action skills; these, in turn, can highlight the need to revise or acquire additional conceptual and domain knowledge. In this sense, the student or manager can master the skills of lifelong learning. While we have emphasized the need to practice action and insight skills, conceptual knowledge also must be constantly exercised; otherwise it will atrophy.

The concept of students as *active* learners, taking charge of their own development, is also central in our framework. This is critical because managers cannot expect to have well-defined programs of "things to learn" as they progress through their careers. Instead, they will be confronted with new problems that require innovative solutions and plans for implementation. Domain knowledge and action skills are the more visible components of managerial performance. However, unless they are grounded in conceptual knowledge and insight skills—both of which are less visible to others—they will not survive as long or generalize as meaningfully in new situations.

Our framework offers insights for other forms of business education aside from the typical two-year MBA program. Both educators and employers can tap this framework as they formulate in-house training plans to foster high-level performance. What knowledge and skills do people lack? How can these best be acquired as employees progress through their careers?

In terms of continuing education programs, we stress

four points. Because the different types of knowledge and skills can become self-reinforcing, our framework first suggests the need to involve both firms and universities in the joint design and delivery of educational programs, and to view these as long-term development. And because both practice and feedback are essential to acquiring skills and knowledge, there is little advantage to short programs unless these are limited to certain specialized topics.

To have the different components of our model reinforce each other, the teaching of conceptual knowledge should be linked directly to the domains in which managers operate. Managers also need to be taught both insight and action skills explicitly because most acquire these haphazardly. And yet, managers have the advantage of being able to practice these skills daily in the workplace. Finally, managers must be empowered to take control of their own development.

These ideas can be applied immediately in executive education programs with "sandwich" structures that intersperse periods of formal schooling and work. In addition to allowing opportunities for practice and feedback, this arrangement allows individuals to share their learning experiences across time. This sharing also facilitates learning from the experiences of others and provides emotional support and reinforcement for the learning process itself.

Executive education is sometimes used to help people *unlearn*. An industry which has long relied on specific domain knowledge may need this process to help employees cope with change caused by new technology or other factors. By focusing on insight skills, or learning the right lessons from experience, such educational programs can help people question what they know and adapt to new realities.

Conclusion

Our goal is to develop people who are smart, savvy, and insightful because these attributes are essential to achieving exceptionally high and consistent levels of performance. To reach this goal requires a partnership between business schools, firms, and students committed to the value of good feedback and continuous improvement of and by the individual.

We conclude with an anecdote. After we had written a first draft of this paper, one of us had lunch with an alumnus who is president of a large U.S. corporation. This executive stated two telling consequences of today's and tomorrow's flatter, less hierarchical organizations. First, it is possible for new employees to make an immediate impact on the organization if they are solution-oriented and effective in presenting and selling their ideas. Influence is based much less upon position and much more on an individual's performance capabilities. It is relatively easy to have access to those with power and budgets. Second, it is now "sink or swim" for the new employee because there is less time and fewer people to mentor others. Immediate performance is not only possible, it is expected.

We believe these comments emphasize the importance of the action and insight skills that we are committed to helping our students acquire. These, however, are not an end in themselves. They improve performance by knowledge acquired during MBA studies as well as the domain knowledge that can be gained through work experience.

A Retrospective and a Look Forward

The question addressed in our selected paper from 1992 can be seen as providing a framework for an investment decision. Specifically, in what activities should a manager invest in order to maximize future career performance? A related issue centered on how business education, both formal and informal, could play a role in this process.

Now, two decades later, the same questions remain relevant. We still see the need for a framework. Indeed, if the manager does not have some clear conceptual ideas to guide his or her development, the consequences of the alternative will be left to chance. It is thus critical that managers play an active role in guiding their own development.

The framework we proposed was inspired by our work in the Booth School's management laboratories as well as theoretical work in psychology and management. We also greatly appreciated the insights underlying the Chicago approach to management education that emphasizes the importance of recognizing that educational institutions have a comparative advantage in providing conceptual knowledge to their students but not in trying to teach domain knowledge that is specific to different areas of business activity.

We felt then, as we do now, that the traditional Chicago approach needed to be augmented with a focus on action and insight skills. A manager may be very knowledgeable, but unless he or she can also take and implement decisions in fast changing environments the probability of success is small. In other words, managers need to develop skills that facilitate the taking of actions and also the ability to learn from experience in domains for which prior exposure to knowledge is insufficient. Formal education goes a long way in developing people who are smart but managers also need to be savvy and insightful. Underlying our approach is the notion that managers should be empowered to take control of their own professional development and that we should help them develop insight skills that would make them effective lifelong learners. Becoming more competent—even wise—at a younger age has real payoff.

When we consider this paper today, we have three reactions. First, we still think that the overall framework makes conceptual sense and are surprised to find that the piece contains several ideas that we have developed in subsequent years (concerning, for example, the nature of intuitive processes). Second, we don't think that the concept of action skills is fully explicated in the original piece. Third (and perhaps related to the second), we are struck by the need to help people find ways of implementing the framework.

So what do we mean by "action skills"? For us, this concept includes the vast array of skills involved in transforming the mental decision to do something into a successful, practical reality. Consider, for example, the decision to launch a new product. In addition to technical and market knowledge, success will depend on a relevant set of actions skills that can involve elements of communication, persuasion, motivating others, teamwork, and so on, which enable the manager to guide the process of implementing the decision. Clearly, different decisions will require different sets of action skills but some might be effective across a range of situations, for example, good communication skills. The important point from our perspective is that every situation provides opportunities to develop action skills. Once managers begin to master the art and science of learning through experience, the processes implied by our framework can become a successful self-fulfilling prophecy.

As in management, the value of our framework should be judged by the extent to which it can be successfully implemented. Over the years, we have talked with managers who have experienced both success and failure in using our ideas. The failures have been largely our fault. We were not fully cognizant of the fact that many managers did not want to acknowledge deficits in their action and insight skills or that these deficits could be reduced through experimentation and practice. We have also often asked managers to do too much within the concepts of the framework, and when effort is not rewarded with immediate success, they are quick to stop trying.

We now believe that successful implementation involves starting with modest learning ambitions but keeping the long-term goal of professional self-development clearly in mind. The work required in strengthening action and insight skills needs to be viewed as an ongoing effort similar in some ways to changing to a healthier life style.

We favor an approach in which, after assessing one's skills, attempts are made to develop at most only two or three skills at a time. Concentrating on a few specific skills has several advantages. First, the learning process is less daunting. Second, one can isolate how one's behavior affects outcomes more clearly. And third, success with one skill can breed success with others. As demonstrated in other areas of management, slow, continuous processes of improvement can have large aggregate effects across time.

To illustrate, a useful trick to remind oneself on a daily basis about needed work on a specific action skill is to embed some mention of it in your e-mail password. Logging on provides a zero-cost reminder to keep the skill salient. When you move on to other skills, change your password! Our colleague and friend Linda Ginzel has brought our framework into many of her classes at Chicago Booth over the past two decades. She advises students that a crucial step in developing insight skills is to actually collect the data of their experiences. Stimulated by writing, this small action replaces the bad habit of simply thinking about taking action. She uses a number of visual devises to remind them to write things down, experiment, and then reflect systematically on the data obtained. The result: people are better able to connect the dots and see patterns and themes in past behavior; they become their own coach.

Two dimensions of learning also motivate the implementation of this framework: fun and competence. As humans, we enjoy activities that are fun, and we are motivated by activities that make us feel more competent. At an attitudinal level, then, we would add to our framework the admonition to seek fun in the process of learning. We make no claim that having fun will guarantee learning the right lessons from experience, but it will undoubtedly increase the probability that you do so and thereby increase your competence.

Notes

[1] This phase also was marked by increased scholarly output by business school faculty.

[2] A. N. Whitehead, *The Aims of Education and Other Essays* (New York: Macmillan, 1929).

[3] G. K. Chesterton, *All Is Grist: A Book of Essays* (New York: Dodd Mead, 1932).

⁴ Excerpted from a talk given in 1956 by James H. Lorie, former associate dean of the Graduate School of Business.

⁵ See, for example, M. T. H. Chi, R. Glaser, and E. Rees, "Expertise in Problem Solving," in *Advances in the Psychology of Human Intelligence*, ed. R. Sternberg (Hillsdale, NJ: Lawrence Erlbaum, 1983).

⁶ Professor Joe Williams, our colleague in the English department at the University of Chicago, makes the point that even experienced lawyers who have learned to write well in a particular specialized domain have considerable difficulty writing well when they change specialties (personal communication, January 1992).

⁷ Roger Peters, *Practical Intelligence* (New York: Harper and Row, 1987), 303.

⁸ See, for example, Alan Mumford, ed., *"Action Learning": A Special Issue in Honour of Reginald W. Revans* (Bradford, England: MCB University Press, 1987).

⁹ For a review of many studies and theories of learning, see E. R. Hilgard and G. H. Bower, *Theories of Learning*, 4th ed. (Englewood Cliffs, NJ: Prentice-Hall, 1975).

¹⁰ See, for example, H. J. Einhorn and R. M. Hogarth, "Confidence in Judgment: Persistence of the Illusion of Validity," *Psychological Review* 85:395–416.

¹¹ L. Eisenberg, "The Social Imperatives of Medical Research," *Science* 198:1106.

¹² The different forms of learning implicit in figures 2 and 3 are similar to what Chris Argyris has referred to as "single loop" and "double loop" learning, respectively. See C. Argyris, "Teaching Smart People How to Learn," *Harvard Business Review* (1991, May-June):99–109.

¹³ W. Durant, *The Story of Philosophy* (New York: Washington Square Press, 1961), 354.

¹⁴ See Argyris, "Teaching Smart People How to Learn."

[15] We are aware that many schools do use criteria other than academic achievement in their selection procedures. However, the self-selecting pool of applicants is heavily biased in favor of those with academic credentials, and academic credentials are given substantial weight in selecting from that self-selecting pool.

.

• 2 •

The Living University

One rarely finds a serious teacher in the absence of serious students. The expectations and hard questions of a demanding student spur a teacher to raise the acceptable standard. Whether one is listed officially as student or as faculty, the chance of intellectual discovery is significantly increased when intense dialogue takes place among members of this community.

Is it not surprising, therefore, that a dialogue so productive is in fact so short-lived? It is as though students swallow a time-release capsule that will later provide useful knowledge on appropriate occasions. From a faculty member's perspective, the emphasis on students early in their careers implies, perhaps, that "old dogs" cannot teach faculty new tricks. Or is it that faculty members view a classroom filled with "clean slates" as part of the ritual of yet another academic year?

Convocation Address, 394th Convocation, University of Chicago, August 24, 1984.

The role of a university in supplying both the private and public sectors with human talent at entry levels is unarguably legitimate. Universities contribute by educating those who will go out and solve problems in the real world. What can be argued, however, is whether a long-term intellectual association between faculty and graduates who are at various stages in their careers outside of the university should be pursued more vigorously.

I will assert that the flow of ideas should be increased in both directions. Universities have a role in influencing the outside world, and the outside world has a role in influencing universities. At the same time, there are barriers that restrict the flow of influence. Academics and practitioners alike tend to erect walls around themselves by way of protection. Any real increase in the dialogue will require changes in both attitudes and behavior. Such changes, or adaptations if you will, are vital to any living organism.

Let me comment first on the benefits of and then on the barriers to productive dialogue.

The Announcements of the Graduate School of Business for the academic year 1916–17 described the need for students to supplement courses dealing with business administration with "such matters as the computing aids of administration." How foreign the 1917 graduate would find today's computing aids! Less dramatic, however, are content changes that continually take place within existing course offerings over relatively short time frames. The stereotype of "yellowed lecture notes" is outdated. Graduates stand to benefit from periodic updates of their formal education.

There is also a need for graduates to acquire new knowledge as their careers develop. Those entering the private sector twenty years ago could not have forecast the extent to which foreign competition would enter the U.S. market with equal or better technology and lower costs, nor that major corporations would be involved in totally new markets with totally new products and services in order to survive and remain profitable. Many past graduates who took jobs in the nonprofit sector of the economy are today involved—often to their dismay—in fierce competitive battles that are hardly distinguishable from those found in the private sector. Nor was it apparent even five years ago that the growth of large centralized business organizations would reverse somewhat and move instead toward smaller, more entrepreneurial units, thereby elevating individuals into general management much earlier in their careers. To cope with these unexpected events, practitioners may need to draw from an entirely different knowledge base than that to which they were exposed as students.

Practitioners also search and invest in order to reduce the amount of trial and error required in managing complex organizations. What else can explain the commercial success of the book *In Search of Excellence?* Both practitioners and academics benefit by studying the kind of questions addressed in this book, namely, what are excellent organizations doing that others are not? Scholars often see a payoff from work on applied problems because such projects may generate ideas of major theoretical significance. The mathematician John von Neumann once reflected:

> I think that it is a relatively good approximation to truth . . . that mathematical ideas originate in empirics, although the genealogy is sometimes long and obscure . . . As a mathematical discipline travels far from its empirical source . . . it is beset with very grave dangers.... Whenever this stage is reached, the only remedy seems to me to be the rejuvenating return to the source.[1]

If these mutual benefits do exist, why then is the dialogue between faculty and university graduates—even between a given institution and its own alumni—not richer and more balanced? At least two barriers come to mind.

First, the knowledge found useful by practitioners may be of a different kind than the knowledge found useful by academics. Some writers have described the difference as one of synthesis versus analysis. Faced with complexity and a frequently unstructured reality, the practitioner moves to bring diverse elements together so as to form a whole. He does this by thinking in analogies, moving constantly back and forth across diverse disciplines, and improvising much like a jazz musician. The analytical process moves in an opposite direction, breaking up the whole into its parts so as to specify relationships, proportions, and the like. The process of discovery here involves model building, quantification, and reliance on a single discipline. The academic views the mixed-up, messy nature of organizational reality as the enemy of scientific induction. The practitioner, on the other hand, may sympathize with George Bernard Shaw's comment: "No man can be a pure specialist without being in the strict sense an idiot."

The difference in defining what knowledge is relevant links closely to a second barrier, and that is the culture of each community. All organizations have patterns of assumptions based on past experiences that serve to define accepted ways of perceiving, thinking, and feeling. The conventional wisdom is filled with exaggerated caricatures of practitioners and academics. For example, the elitist stereotype of the latter group has a long history that is vividly illustrated by the attitude of an Oxford professor some one hundred years ago: "The advantages of a classical education," he wrote, "are two-fold. It enables us to look down with contempt on those who have not shared its advantages and also fits us for places of emolument, not only in this world but in that which is to come." [2] Attempts to fuse the two cultures generate negative reactions—the accusation of "selling out" or the question, "if you're so smart, then why aren't you rich?"

Some differences in structure and attitude are both real and important for maintaining the distinctive competence of each culture. Other differences are merely myths that serve to retard meaningful dialogue. There is little difference between practitioner and scientist in the basic entrepreneurial act—both share a certain skepticism and an open-mindedness toward new concepts and techniques. Some of the best scholars I know are found in nonacademic settings. The task of education is not a monopoly of universities. Organizations are very much involved with education since coaching, mentoring, and teaching are important parts of the job of every manager. Thus, it is bizarre to think that students without organizational affiliations are embraced as full partners in this intellectual community only to become somehow transformed and therefore suspect after assuming the practitioner role.

Those responsible for the future of a living university have the challenge of finding ways to lower these barriers. The motivation for initiating new channels to the outside world should be far deeper than simply replacing one source of funding with another. Stronger links will help us get on with the job of innovation, and that is, after all, what we are about. There is great value to the flow of knowledge and ideas across the artificial boundaries of subjects, disciplines, and professions. Not only are problems in one field often solved by insights from another, but the pooling of all these skills and interests encourages a process of intellectual fermentation. Stronger links will also help us reduce the risk of becoming isolated. In many fields, it is now far easier for practitioners to get to sources of knowledge than it is for academics to get to sources of action.

When my children were young, I used to read them a book by Shel Silverstein entitled *The Giving Tree*. The story describes the touching relationship between a boy and an apple tree throughout the boy's life. The boy takes everything from the tree—its leaves, its branches, and finally even its trunk—without giving much in return. There are some parallels in the academic community. Undergraduates ask for tuition support. Graduate students seek fellowships. Faculty want grants and lighter teaching loads.

In my opinion, the first step in building this needed dialogue should be taken by the academic community. The more we know, understand, and care for persons and organizations on the outside, the greater is the chance that we will be helpful. And when meaningful expertise has been shared with the outside world, much will be returned.

Notes

[1] John von Neumann, "The Mathematician," in *Works of the Mind,* vol. 1, no. 1 (Chicago: University of Chicago Press, 1947), 195–196.

[2] Sir Adrian Cadbury, "Partnership between Education and Business," in *Education in the Age of Information: The Challenge of Technology,* ed. Carl Payne (Manchester, England: Manchester University Press, 1993), 55.

Breaking Rules *and* Following Rules

I know that it's dangerous to make predictions as to exactly how and when any new program will have its impact. I developed a laboratory in new product development in the business school in 1978 and ran it for seventeen years. Teams of ten to twelve students would work to develop a product or service for a sponsoring company over a period of six months. The laboratory had the expected impact of generating many new products, a number of which were actually commercialized by companies. Students learned a good deal about the real work of developing new products and acquired useful teamwork skills. But, quite unexpectedly, the intense work resulted in seven marriages and at last count thirteen children. That's quintessential new product development,

Keynote address given for the opening of the Executive MBA Program in Singapore on September 15, 2000. The address was included in the program for the Management Conference Asia 2000 sponsored by the University of Chicago Graduate School of Business, Shangri-La Hotel, Singapore.

and for these seven couples, I'm sure more memorable than what happened in class.

One of the joys of being a professor is having time, particularly during the summer, to read. I read a lot this summer—novels, biographies, books written by experienced business people and journalists, some poetry, books in the biological and social sciences, including Bob Fogel's *The Fourth Great Awakening*, which I would heartily recommend.[1] This summer's reading was quite a feast.

There were two books—clearly *not* in the business category—that struck me as containing useful insights for my own thinking about creativity and innovation in business.

I very much like drawing ideas from domains other than business because metaphorical thinking gets me out of ruts and shines light in places that otherwise would remain in the shadows. Metaphors tend to "level the playing field" in working toward fresh solutions because they are welcoming to people from diverse backgrounds and technical expertise. Metaphors are used widely in the liberal arts and as such are an art that liberates—that encourages exploration and the fun of seeing things in new ways.

I'll begin with a short overview of Gunther Schuller's new book on orchestral conducting, which was a gift from a Chicago alumnus and good friend who, incidentally, studied philosophy as an undergraduate.[2] Schuller himself is a distinguished composer, horn player, and conductor. He begins with a short quote from the poet T. S. Eliot. Eliot writes:

A struggle, more or less unconscious, between the creator and the interpreter is almost inevitable. The interest of a performer is almost certain to be centered in himself.[3]

Following from this idea, Schuller then presents a lot of empirical data showing that in his judgment modern-day orchestra conductors pay too little attention to the musical scores of widely performed composers such as Beethoven, Brahms, or Bartok and blatantly ignore many of these composers' own markings on the score for dynamics, tempo, and so on.

By the conductor's own behavior, it is as if he is saying to the players and to the audience:

"I'm more important than the composer."
"I don't fully trust what the composer wrote."
"I know what he meant."
"I'll make it better."
"Follow my lead."

According to Schuller, this attitude is driven not just from the enormous power embedded in the role of conductor but also from a desire to differentiate one conductor from another. Conductors learn that they will stand out— be more noteworthy (even make more money, perhaps)—if their recording of Beethoven's Third Symphony, for example, differs from someone else's recording of that same symphony.

Schuller then suggests three things that an accomplished conductor should do:

> 1. first, trust and respect the composer; after all, it's the composer who is the creator;
>
> 2. know all there is to know about a score, down to the most miniscule details; and
>
> 3. develop the necessary skills to transmit that information to the players within the orchestra so that together they can realize the work.

The core idea here is that creativity must operate within limits. Schuller describes the process in the following terms:

> The secret of great artistry and true integrity of interpretation lies in the ability to bring to life the score . . . with the fullest knowledge of that score, so that the conductor's personality expresses itself creatively within the parameters of the score.[4]

In this spirit, then, I am going to maintain that careful attention to a composer's score is one important source of inspiration and innovation not only in music but also in business.

I'll use an example that's very timely given the inauguration of the Executive MBA Program in Singapore, namely, the original "musical score," if you will, for the University of Chicago.

The visionary founder of the university, William Rainey Harper, wrote in 1892 about the ways in which Chicago should differ from other universities. He had a bold vision right from the beginning, particularly when benchmarked against the financial resources that were then available to him.

In his view, research and the training of scholars to pursue research were at the core of the University of Chicago. Within this core, he set forth values that included the importance of concentration in a faculty member's teaching and in a student's course schedule, flexibility of the curriculum, and respect for the individual.

But beyond these ideas, and highly unusual in that era, was Harper's belief in extending the intellectual excitement of the university to a much broader community. Harper wanted the university to reach out beyond its Gothic walls to make its unique *brand* of education available to anyone who could profit by it. And an important part of his vision was that in extending the university's reach, it must not compromise academic standards. To this end, he insisted on using the regular tenured faculty, demanding the same workload as for students taking classes on campus, and giving academic credit for their work.

Harper's idea (some said folly) was more than just an idea. Under his leadership, the university immediately began a wide range of extension efforts, including affiliations with smaller colleges throughout the United States, correspondence courses, the University of Chicago Press, evening classes in downtown Chicago, and public lectures by regular faculty in cities and towns west of Chicago.

The year 2000 is a different era, of course. Travel to Singapore from Chicago is now about twenty-two hours. In 1892 when Harper crafted this vision of reaching out to the larger community, twenty-two hours on a train headed west toward Los Angeles would get the traveler only to Hutchinson, Kansas, a mere 692 miles from Chicago, or to Little Falls, Minnesota (580 miles from Chicago), if one were heading west toward Seattle.

But while transportation technology has evolved, I think it's instructive and critical for today's interpreters of his vision to explore whether Harper would find the university's presence in Singapore consistent with his vision.

The answer to me is clear. The Executive MBA Program is clearly innovative (no other institution in the world is attempting something this bold, particularly with the exchanges among the Asian, North American, and European campuses). At the same time, this initiative is totally consistent with the university's one-hundred-plus-year mission. Harper's only surprise would be that in twenty-two hours the faculty could get to the other side of the globe rather than down the railroad track to Kansas or Minnesota!

Thus leaders of organizations can, and should, encourage employees to search for new ideas within an organization's existing script. Similar to Shakespeare or Beethoven, old scripts and melodies can continue to have great value in the current, changing business environment. These scores have plenty of space for continued innovation.

However, I find resistance to this idea. Recent books on business seem to sell because of clever titles about change, revolution, or the value of throwing out the past. Geoffrey Moore's recent book entitled *Inside the Tornado* conjures up images of destruction.[5] Gary Hamel titles his new book *Leading the Revolution* and makes a bold statement that "a company that is evolving slowly is already on its way to extinction."[6]

This theme of rejecting the past has a very long history. Some of you may recall Thoreau's advice at the opening of *Walden,* published in the mid-1800s. He wrote:

> Practically, the old have no very important advice to give the young . . . I have lived some thirty years on this planet, and I have yet to hear the first syllable of valuable or even earnest advice from my seniors. . . . Here is life, an experiment to a great extent untried by me; but it does not avail me that they have tried it.[7]

While we might applaud Thoreau's resistance to blind conformity, I do think that leaders need to insist that people within their organizations look very carefully at early scripts written and talked about by the founders for clues about future innovations. It's productive to explore the past to discover useful ideas for the future.

Let me turn now to a second book that I think provides some insight into unlocking innovation within organizations, and that is Leslie Stainton's recent biography of the Spanish poet, musician, artist, playwright, and director Federico García Lorca.[8] The story of his life provides a very different perspective on innovation.

García Lorca was born into a bourgeois family in Granada in 1898. Despite this traditional upbringing and criticism from his father, he was always at the edge—constantly experimenting, creating, and playing with new ideas. To him, rules were for the mediocre. He asked:

> How are you going to lock one person's heart inside a prison belonging to somebody else? How can someone flaunt the splendid wings that God has placed on their shoulders?[9]

Not surprisingly, he found much of what was going on in Spanish theater at the time to be lacking. His vision as a playwright was to create what he termed "theater beneath the sand," in which audiences would engage with the tragic, the real, and their own fears. He would say: "I want to take topics and problems that people are afraid of confronting and put them onstage."[10]

García Lorca was a veritable fountain of ideas, many of which never materialized. His disregard for deadlines was the source of enormous frustration among those with whom he worked. He once told a reporter that he was at work on approximately 4,595 projects. Of those, he said, he'd write only four at the most.

His life and work was one of constant experimentation. He continued moving back and forth between Madrid and Granada and also spent periods of time in New York and Buenos Aires. He experimented with puppet theater and street theater and gave public lectures on many different topics.

Throughout his life, he had the support and opportunity to collaborate with a community of like-minded people, including the composer Manuel de Falla, the artist Salvador Dalí, various theater directors, and other young people who would regularly sit together and talk throughout the night.

But as is true with many rule breakers, García Lorca acquired enemies because of the nature of his plays and poems and his personal style. His plays were sometimes described as crude, immoral, irreverent—an affront to honorable and decent people. Following a short interview, one journalist described García Lorca as "a conceited fool . . . and a little charlatan." The ultimate enemy turned out to be profascist soldiers at the beginning of the Spanish Civil War; on the morning of August 18, 1936, at the age of only thirty-nine, he was shot to death by a firing squad.

When I finished reading this book, I found myself thinking about parallels in the work of the economist Joseph Schumpeter. Defining the entrepreneurial function in business, he wrote:

> To understand new things is difficult and constitutes a distinct economic function, first, because new things lie outside the routine tasks which everyone understands. Secondly, the environment resists new things in ways that range from simple refusal either to finance or buy, to physical attack on the man who tries to produce it.[11]

So just as innovation flows from opportunities associated with the existing script of the business, it's also true that rule breaking is another important source of innovation.

We have all experienced, I suppose, the difficulty of successful rule breaking, particularly within organizations that are successful. One often finds here a culture of success that also includes shame associated with any kind of failure. Lots of creative energy is devoted to making the status quo legitimate and putting in place a "don't screw it up" mentality. And as a consequence, more time may be devoted to satisfying the needs of those within the company—the internal marketplace so to speak—than finding and exploiting opportunities in the company's external marketplace. (It's somewhat ironic that the same firm that espouses great admiration for the free market employs a central planning paradigm to run their own operations!)

I like to think of the successful business as similar to a theater company that specializes in performing the works of one playwright such as Molière or Shakespeare. Such a company can deliver extraordinary performances because members of the company know who to hire and put into which roles, they have directors who know how to stage productions, and they understand the particular needs and wants of their audience.

But the same company that performs well in staging the work of one playwright often has difficulty accommodating other scripts, other styles of directing or acting, and performing in front of different audiences. Put simply, the tightly scripted, specialized company often doesn't have enough variation in its human capital to do really new things. They've only hired people who were quick to learn the dominant script and gotten rid of people who refused to do what they were told to do or were slow to learn the script. They've structured training such that those who have been around for a long time teach those who are recently arrived; it would never occur to senior management that some of the teaching should go in the opposite direction. Because of the discomfort that's generated by weird ideas or weird people, it's unlikely that there are any Federico García Lorcas on their payrolls. Is it any wonder then that finding new opportunities outside of the existing script is so difficult?

If you'll just bear with me for a moment, let me push the theater metaphor a bit further. Imagine, if you will, companies becoming more like repertory theaters with a permanent set of actors, directors, and set designers who have the ability to mount a varied selection of plays—some coming from the classical repertory, others from contemporary playwrights, and still others that are improvisational in nature.

Mounting a diversity of productions of this sort clearly requires a very different mindset about innovation than if one were just performing the work of one playwright, however creative that work might be. Ideas for new plays can come from many different sources at unexpected times and in unexpected ways. The source of ideas is difficult, if not impossible, to predict ex-ante.

In the business context, then, if senior managers are looking for innovation outside of the existing business, new processes are needed that can exist independently of—and be shielded from—the normal channels for getting things done. Ideas shouldn't have to share a channel with today's price of raw materials, fear of product liability suits, or the annual report.

An example of one such process that you may find interesting is what I've termed the internal venture marketplace. Think of this market as a regularly scheduled event that gives employees an opportunity to display new business concepts, prototypes, or business plans in a public forum within a company. (You may want to think about it as a street market that sets up, displays things for sale, transacts with buyers, and then closes down.) The sellers, who are employees, compete aggressively for seed money from buyers first within the company and in some cases later from sources outside the company.

The atmosphere of the internal marketplace has some of the characteristics that I earlier described in García Lorca's short life. Employees have opportunities to perform and build prototypes rather than sitting around in windowless conference rooms simply talking about new ideas. A venture marketplace encourages experimentation—getting things almost right without the need to worry about being perfect. There's time pressure and a healthy dose of competitiveness given that some projects will receive funding and others will not. Like the economist's perfect market, there are no barriers to entry. Because anyone in the organization can play, a lot of ideas will likely be generated. And, like a real market, the projects that have the greatest commercial potential will get funded and attract others to participate. Quality work will flourish while less-interesting ideas will appropriately wither.

We can already see some examples of large companies beginning to move in this direction. J. P. Morgan has created a unit called LabMorgan that will spend up to $1 billion on new initiatives in 2000. Interestingly, it has received many e-finance business plans, a fifth of which come from inside J. P. Morgan.

In Germany, Siemens recently conducted a business plan competition in its semiconductor unit. All employees who wanted to take part in the competition were allowed to do so, and more than two hundred teams submitted proposals. Several dozen were developed into detailed business plans, with five businesses finally emerging as viable candidates for seed funding.

Can creative initiatives emerge from *following* rules—adhering to the old script? Can creative initiatives emerge from *breaking* rules—writing new scripts? I've said that the answer to both questions is "yes."

When I reflect on the leadership challenges associated with answering "yes" to both of these questions, two words come to mind: *courage* and *paradox*.

It takes courage to innovate in both of these ways. As a leader, one has to resist being dragged into a middle ground somewhere between the old and new scripts. It is the leader's role to study the existing script, to know it well, and to communicate this reality to others. Without courage, it's all too easy to slowly drift away from fundamental beliefs and values. It is also the leader's role to protect those who are working to create new scripts from attacks from others who fear change or resist looking at the market with new lenses. It takes courage to keep really new exploration from being derailed either intentionally or unintentionally.

Courage often translates into setting boundaries that are needed for successful innovation. Ken Melrose, who is CEO of the Toro Company, claims that he spends a lot of time setting appropriate boundaries within which to consider various growth strategies.

> People need to be continually reminded about Toro's "playing field." We are a lawn-care, not a lawn-mower company, our quality must be higher than our competition, and Toro dealers are a critical component of our success. When our growth initiatives have respected these factors, the chance of successful new initiatives is good. When we have tried to innovate outside of these factors, we have most often failed. So, my role in the area of strategy and innovation is often saying "No" to well-meaning people.[12]

Creativity thrives when people play within well understood and accepted boundaries. In jazz, everyone must agree on the key, chord progression, and simple melodic line. All of these elements are nonnegotiable. Yet within these constraints, creative improvisation can flourish. Boundaries provide a sense of security, and security is an important underpinning of creativity.

The second word that comes to mind in viewing these two sources of innovation is *paradox*. Is it easy for a leader to focus a company's energy and resources on its original script in order to find new opportunities and *simultaneously* create an environment that encourages new scripts which may be hostile to the existing order? I don't think this is easy since it requires holding in tension two different (and seemingly inconsistent) perspectives. Yet, there's a genius in being able to have both A *and* B rather having to choose between A *or* B. The "genius of the *and*" can increase a company's repertoire of skills. And having access to more skills increases agility that can be highly strategic in a world moving so quickly and with such uncertainty.

I find it important to note that creative leaders often behave in seemingly paradoxical ways and are comfortable doing so. The late Nobel laureate Richard Feynman, besides being a physicist, was at various times a repairer of radios, a picker of locks, an artist, a dancer, a bongo player, and even a decipherer of Mayan hieroglyphics. Perpetually curious about the world, he was an exemplary empiricist. Could his comfort with multiple identities—the discipline of both focus *and* agility—be a model for creative business leadership as we look forward?

Personally, I'd put a lot of money on the bet that it will be.

Notes

[1] Robert W. Fogel, *The Fourth Great Awakening* (Chicago: University of Chicago Press, 2000).

[2] Gunther Schuller, *The Compleat Conductor* (Oxford, England: Oxford University Press, 1997).

[3] T. S. Eliot, "The Possibility of a Poetic Drama," in *The Sacred Wood*, 3rd edition (London: Methuen and Co., 1932), 69.

[4] Schuller, *The Compleat Conductor*, 24.

[5] Geoffrey A. Moore, *Inside the Tornado: Strategies for Developing, Leveraging, and Surviving Hypergrowth Markets* (New York: Harper Collins, 1995).

[6] Gary Hamel, *Leading the Revolution* (Cambridge, MA: Harvard Business School Press, 2000).

[7] Henry David Thoreau, *Walden* (New York: Penguin Books, 1985), 329–330.

[8] Leslie Stainton, *Lorca: A Dream of Life* (New York: Farrar, Straus and Giroux, 1999).

[9] Ibid., 47.

[10] Ibid., 250.

[11] Joseph A. Schumpeter, *Capitalism, Socialism and Democracy* (San Francisco: Harper Perennial, 2008), 132.

[12] From an unpublished talk by Ken Melrose to an MBA class at the Chicago Booth School of Business.

·4·

The Compleat Strategist

My work on this talk began last June 26, when I had dinner with a good friend, Ed Miller, who is a 1983 graduate of the Graduate School of Business. Knowing my interest in music, Ed kindly gave me a book by the well-known composer and conductor Gunther Schuller titled *The Compleat Conductor*.[1]

I was intrigued with the title of this book for reasons that went beyond music and conducting.

I was intrigued first with the Old English spelling of the word *complete*, which reminded me of an earlier version of the course catalogue for the university's Extension Division that for many years was called *The Compleat Gargoyle*. (It brought back a conversation with a wonderful human be-

Keynote address given on October 6, 2000, at the 5th Annual Alumni Event sponsored by the University of Chicago, Graduate School of Business, Sheraton Chicago Hotel. I wish to acknowledge some very helpful conversations with R. Craig Burlington, Ernest F. Fiske, and Barbara Lanebrown in preparing this speech. P. G. Stanwood's recent book, *Izaak Walton* (Twayne Publishers, 1998), is filled with insights into Walton's life and approach, and I have woven some of these into my remarks.

ing named Margaret Fallers who was an associate provost of the university. Margaret took pleasure in sharing with others that one of her greatest joys was perusing *The Compleat Gargoyle* cover to cover while lounging in the bathtub.)

I was also intrigued with the fact that the spelling of the word *compleat* was labeled "archaic" in the *Oxford English Dictionary*. Perhaps it's my nature, but I've always been attracted to places where others are not, because out-of-the-way venues have quite often yielded unanticipated gifts.

And finally, I suppose, I was intrigued with the book's title because I had just finished teaching two sections of a course on business strategy in the spring quarter and was thinking to myself what, if anything, would I do differently over the ten weeks of the quarter if I were to change the title of the course from Business Policy to The Compleat Strategist?

I began in early July by typing the archaic word *compleat* into the search engine at Amazon.com. (Talk about paradox!) Sure enough, there were a number of recently published books using the Old English spelling of the word *complete* in the title. There were ninety-four listings to be precise. In the spirit of Hollywood's sequel movies, *The Compleat Day Trader II* seemed interesting, but I didn't order it.[2]

I did, however, order a book with the long title *The Compleat Cockroach: A Comprehensive Guide to the Most Despised (and Least Understood) Creature on Earth.*[3] I thought this guide might be interesting for business strategists since cockroaches have been around for more than 300 million years—considerably longer than the 150-year-old companies studied by Collins and Porras in their best-selling book, *Built to Last*.[4] Cockroaches have witnessed the emergence *and* disappearance of the dinosaurs and continue to thrive despite an estimated quarter of a billion dollars spent annually in the United States to get rid of them. If strategy is about staying in the game, perhaps the cockroach has something important to teach us.

Throughout all of my wanderings around the word *compleat*, one book continued to surface—one that I suppose could be considered the grandfather of all books bearing the word *compleat*—and that is Izaak Walton's celebrated *The Compleat Angler*, first published in 1653 when he was sixty years old.[5] I paid attention to this book not only because of the word *compleat*, but also because it rivals the Holy Bible in popularity if the number of translations and editions are any measure of renown. Surely, I thought, there must be something to learn from a product with that much staying power! And I wondered whether it might contain some voices from the past that could illuminate the present.

For those of you who have not read *The Compleat Angler*, Walton casts the story in the form of a dialogue occurring over several days in the English countryside. Each day ends up at an alehouse with a good meal and drink followed by communal poetry and singing. Walton takes the role of a fisherman and throughout twenty-one chapters guides a willing student, who was a one-time hunter, through the fine points of effective fishing.

A number of ideas relevant to the compleat strategist immediately jumped out as I read this book for the first time.

First, I thought it fascinating that Walton himself was a compulsive tinkerer. *The Compleat Angler* went through four subsequent editions over the two decades following its initial publication. To call each new edition of this book a revision really misses the point. Each new edition underwent extensive remodeling. One of Walton's admirers, in fact, describes the process that he went through as an exercise in the "art of assemblage."

I think that the compleat strategist might well be an unabashed tinkerer like Walton. It makes sense to think of strategy as an evolving assemblage—something akin to what I observed my five-year-old grandson doing last weekend when playing with Legos. He kept building new and more interesting structures using essentially the same pieces. Tinkering captures the idea that strategy often emerges from actions, in addition to being something that is planned and deliberate. Tinkering also makes it legitimate to get things almost right and gives permission to send the perfectionist inside each of us off to take a nap.

Another insight into strategy comes from the fact that Walton borrowed heavily from other sources in writing *The Compleat Angler*. He imitated and, shockingly to some, even plagiarized. It turns out that another manual on fishing was published some eighty years prior to Walton's. It, too, featured a dialogue between a fisherman and a student. I should say that making use of others' material was not uncommon in Walton's time, and writers have a long history, as William Faulkner once said, of working with anything useful that's not nailed down. What Walton added, which was missing in the earlier guide, was a more engaging dialogue *and* a setting that connected deeply with nature.

The compleat strategist, I want to argue, must also have an inclination to imitate others' strategies, to use any ideas that are not nailed down. Jazz musicians often learn their craft by imitating early recordings of players they admire. Imitation in jazz is the first step toward creative expression. New expression is to be found in the details, in the nuances of performance.

The success of Walton's book over three centuries also suggested a third quality of the compleat strategist—and that is the ability to fashion and tell a good story. Walton introduces recurring story lines. For example, there's the repeated dialogue between the fisherman and his student—first a formal debate between the two, then conversion of the skeptic, followed by willing instruction on how to master a particular technique. The book is also filled with what we today label "fish stories." Even his coauthor writing in the final 1679 edition of *The Compleat Angler* suggested that Walton's advice for catching a big trout would likely produce no other outcome than losing the fish.

Good strategies *are* good stories, and good strategists *are* good storytellers. Stories are large containers that can hold facts and fantasies, both of which I believe are essential in crafting a compelling strategy. People within an organization are more likely to buy into a story of the business and its future that's well told than they are to buy into a deck of PowerPoint slides.

A case in point is the perspective of James Billington, who at the time of Ronald Reagan's retirement was Librarian of Congress. In an after-dinner speech, he said:

> The President's ability as a raconteur helped him deal with the Soviets. Mr. Reagan saw America as a wonderful story with a simple vision not intelligible to foreign policy wonks. The Soviets saw themselves as part of a static, unrealistic theory. The Cold War was a victory of story over theory.[6]

So, these were the three qualities of the compleat strategist that jumped out at me on a first reading of Walton's book:

- tinkering,
- imitating, and
- storytelling.

But during the month of August, I kept pondering whether these three qualities would be enough to warrant the title of compleat strategist. I concluded that these were not enough and that there were at least two additional qualities that should be added. These qualities have to do with being smart in ways different from how "smarts" are usually measured. These two qualities have more to do with innate characteristics of individuals and less to do with what has been acquired through formal education or experience.

I call the first of these an open vision and the second, personal philosophy.

Let me go back again to *The Compleat Angler* and explore the idea of an open vision. Walton draws a very large circle around the subject of fishing:

- He writes about many different species of fish, including fascinating tidbits about their history.

- He provides detailed advice on catching fish, recommending a different technique for each type and different techniques for catching the same fish in different seasons of the year.

- He travels *backward* in the value chain, so to speak, and provides detailed instructions on building fishponds, making artificial flies, baiting the hook, choosing the right worm for the right fish, and making and then dyeing the fishing line itself.

- Then he travels *forward* in the value chain, giving detailed instructions for preparing fish. Some of his recipes read like those in *Gourmet* magazine.

Why is drawing such a large circle important for the compleat strategist? In the first place let me suggest that an open
vision helps strategic thinking by sensing patterns and weak
signals that others may not see and by avoiding observation-
al ruts. An open vision is an antidote to reading the same
business publications, focusing on the same best practices,
or talking about differentiation while, in reality, investing in
more of the same. Like *The Compleat Angler*, an open vision
helps a strategist discover bits and pieces, peculiar idiosyncratic elements in the environment that may help snag more
customers.

And luckily, there's much evidence to suggest that we all
have the ability to widen our vision despite years of education and experience that often reward memorization and
conformity more than true exploration. John Stilgoe, a professor of history at Harvard, puts it well:

> Exploration is second nature, a second nature in-
> timately linked to the adolescent days of tattered
> sneakers and old Raleigh bicycles, a second nature
> lost in these turn-of-the-millennium days, but a
> second nature easy enough to recover any weekday
> evening, any Sunday morning, any hour snatched
> away from programmed learning, from the webs
> and nets that invisibly and insidiously snare.[7]

There's also a second reason why an open vision is an

essential quality for the compleat strategist. I have always agreed with Leo Burnett's view that good advertising people understand the "fitness of things." I think about his idea of the "fitness of things" as understanding whether a given strategy really fits a company's capabilities. Now, I don't know about your experience, but I am perplexed when I witness an otherwise good strategy being forced on an organization that lacks the skills or desire to implement it consistently. It's like a transplant that will simply be rejected.

In this regard, someone who wants to become a compleat strategist might well take a look at the world of the performing arts. It's not an accident that great playwrights such as Shakespeare and Molière wrote with particular actors in mind. Nor is it an accident that Duke Ellington wrote with particular musicians in mind. Ellington once said:

> You can't write music right unless you know how the man that'll play it plays poker. You've got to write with certain men in mind. You write just for their abilities and natural tendencies and give them places where they do their best.[8]

Let me turn, finally, to the second quality, which I've called personal philosophy, and suggest to you that *this* is the foundation for becoming a compleat strategist. It's the essential ingredient, I believe, because personal philosophy bridges the gap between practical techniques and human values. I think of philosophy as a personal story or point of view—one's current definition about how the world works, what motivates its actors, what one considers to be meaningful values and meaningful outcomes.

Going back to Walton for just a moment, those who have studied his life and writings argue that had it not been for the English Civil War, *The Compleat Angler* would not have been written. The ten years prior to its publication had been chaotic. King Charles had fled London along with many members of Parliament and the Anglican clergy. It was a time when one had to choose sides, and Walton, who also fled London, sided with the royalists.

The Compleat Angler, then, can be thought of as a description of life—a vision, if you will—that no longer existed when it was written. His vision (naïve as it may have been) was that of a gentle, fresh, spring countryside with rivers filled with fish anxious to be caught and eaten. All of the characters in the book model values of simplicity, endurance, contemplation, and even good manners. Those fish stories that have led generations of hopeful fisherman to buy this book are undoubtedly less important in explaining its continued sales than the book's larger fish story about how to maintain optimism in a difficult world.

I'm clearly not suggesting that Walton's particular philosophy is necessarily that which is relevant to business strategy. A gentle, pastoral setting hardly characterizes today's business environment. But philosophy is bedrock for the compleat strategist, and I would argue that *it* is the source of real uniqueness because it stems from idiosyncratic qualities that each one of us possesses. It's both genuine and authentic, and hard to copy.

Mozart once reflected on his own uniqueness in a letter. He wrote:

> Why my productions take from my hand that particular form and style that makes them different from the works of other composers, is probably owing to the same cause which renders my nose so large, or in short, makes it Mozart's, and different from those of other people. For I really do not study or aim at any originality.[9]

So, I would argue that a personal philosophy, though not always made explicit, underlies personal and organizational strategies.

In the case of the University of Chicago, for example, its first president, William Rainey Harper, held a philosophy about people and learning. He believed that those who wanted to learn and had the capacity for learning should have access to the university's faculty even if they couldn't study full-time on campus. I like to think that the Gleacher Center in downtown Chicago and our new campuses in Barcelona and Singapore are examples of Harper's personal philosophy made tangible a century later.

Alfred Sloan's personal philosophy included a view of business as a deeply spiritual undertaking, enormously powerful and, accordingly, with the ability to do great good, not only for shareholders but also for the nation as a whole. His philosophy was a celebration of the American enterprise system, and it helps to explain GM's growth, decision-making processes, and market dominance.

A more recent example might be the much-discussed Herb Kelleher of Southwest Airlines. He operates from a philosophy about work that says, among other things: "If it's not fun, why do it?" This perspective has a lot to do with decisions about who to hire which tie directly to Southwest's emphasis on customer satisfaction. His philosophy also shapes the kind of messages he sends to employees, such as: "The customer is not always right."

In recent days I've found myself asking what's missing in Chicago's MBA program and in most others for that matter. I think it is this. These programs focus on the acquisition of tools and concepts without giving enough attention to the container that holds them—that is, not enough attention to helping people surface and reflect upon their own values and personal philosophy. I realize now in October that I must work hard on this issue in the coming days as I prepare my strategy courses for the winter quarter.

I can't resist ending these remarks in the same way that Izaak Walton ended the last chapter of *The Compleat Angler* with these words:

I have almost tired my self, and I fear more than almost tired you: but I now see Tottenham High-Cross, and our short walk thither shall put a period to my too long discourse . . . Therefore, my advice is that you endeavor to be honestly rich, or contentedly poor; but be sure that your riches be justly got, or you spoil all.

Notes

[1] Gunther Schuller, *The Compleat Conductor* (Oxford, England: Oxford University Press, 1997).

[2] Jake Bernstein, *The Compleat Day Trader II* (New York: McGraw-Hill, 1998).

[3] David George Gordon, *The Compleat Cockroach: A Comprehensive Guide to the Most Despised (and Least Understood) Creature on Earth* (Berkeley, CA: Ten Speed Press, 1996).

[4] Jim Collins and Jerry I. Porras, *Built to Last: Successful Habits of Visionary Companies* (New York: HarperCollins, 1997).

[5] Izaak Walton and Charles Cotton, *The Compleat Angler, or The Contemplative Man's Recreation* (New York: Modern Library, 1998).

[6] Patrick Butters, "A Believer with a Simple Vision: Stalwarts Gather to Honor Reagan," *Washington Times,* September 29, 1997.

[7] John R. Stilgoe, *Outside Lies Magic* (New York: Walker and Company, 1998).

[8] John Edward Hasse, *The Life and Genius of Duke Ellington* (Cambridge, MA: Da Capo Press 1995), 84.

[9] Edward Holmes, *The Life of Mozart* (New York: Everyman's Library, 1992).

·5·

The Professional and the Amateur

Let me share with you a story that begins almost one hundred years ago. It involves the start-up of a new agency selling life insurance that grew over its first twenty years to become one of the largest and most profitable in the United States.

Business success rarely has a single cause and this story is no exception. Certainly one factor was timing. The first thirty years of the twentieth century witnessed the evolution of life insurance from a luxury purchased by the wealthy to a necessity sought out by broad segments of the population.

But this company grew faster than other agencies. That's because it more aggressively recruited new agents, trained these agents thoroughly, created innovative insurance products, and provided agents with highly persuasive sales materials. In today's jargon we would say that the company better understood and executed its business model.

Convocation Address, 465th Convocation, University of Chicago, June 10, 2001.

Of course, you can't overlook the talents of those in leadership positions, and similar to the stories of HP, Intel, and Apple, the two founders of this new agency had complementary skills. One partner was extroverted, good with numbers and operational details, and comfortable in representing the agency in front of prospective agents. The other was more introverted—even shy—but filled with new ideas and skillful at conveying those ideas in straightforward prose.

These three factors—strong leadership, the right business model, and fortuitous timing—seem as relevant today as they were in 1907. The name of this company was Ives and Myrick.

There is another plotline to this story, however, a sort of a footnote. One of the two founders pursued a passion for music as a pastime. He composed music in the evenings, on weekends, walking to and from work, and sometimes even stole a few moments at the office. During the same time that he was building the company, he was also writing music with no audience in mind, with no guarantee of ever hearing his compositions performed, and certainly with no expectation of monetary reward.

This footnote to the story turns out to be *the* story, and his business career becomes the footnote. For this workaday insurance man was Charles Ives, who is considered by many to be America's first great composer. His pastime, not his paid work, became his legacy.

The University of Chicago's Andrew Abbott begins his

book, *The System of Professions*: "The professions dominate our world. They heal our bodies, measure our profits, save our souls."[1] I happen to agree with Abbott's thesis. The word *professional* is pervasive and used widely to entice customers, clients, patients, and even students. (I noticed, for example, an ad for the GMC Envoy that begins: "From Professional Grade People Come Professional Grade SUVs. We are Professional Grade." How could anyone resist with all that professionalism!) Even truckers are attracted to the word. A semi that I passed while driving to the university last week was emblazoned with the phrase: "Pulling for America with [you guessed it] Professional Pride."

I have great respect for the professions. How could I *not* as I stand here at the finest professional school in the world? According to a commonly recognized definition, a professional is someone in possession of a body of theoretical knowledge and the art of applying it.

Thus, G. K. Chesterton reminds us to cry out for the person who is skilled in the scientific parts of a trade when a problem is serious.[2] Get the person with the theoretical knowledge. While this person might be labeled *unpractical,* he or she will turn out to be indispensable.

Countless graduates of this institution have demonstrated the payoff from high levels of scientific insight and integrity and from having the intellectual rigor to distinguish between noise and what is really important and enduring.

But it is worth noting that while the word *professional* has enjoyed wider and wider usage and has developed increasingly positive connotations in the English language, its opposite—the word *amateur*—has suffered over time. (Can you imagine, for example, telling your friends and employers that you've just graduated from the GSB and are proud to be a business amateur?)

Amateurs are often derided as dabblers, second-rate people who tackle things superficially and without professional skills. But the dictionary also provides another definition of *amateur* derived from the Latin term for someone who works at an art or science for its own pleasure. It is this definition that Professor Emeritus Wayne Booth uses in his delightful book on being an amateur, titled *For the Love of It.*[3]

Two questions come to my mind when I reflect on professional and amateur pursuits.

First, why is it that we feel the need to choose one *or* the other? That is, why do we feel compelled to choose between one way that evaluates the worth of any activity according to its future benefit relative to its cost (in expected value terms) and another way where being fully present in the moment overrides any serious concern about future payoffs?

After all, the differences between these two heuristics aren't really all that large when it comes to the work itself. Master chefs do not have a monopoly on well-grilled steaks. Both amateurs and professionals participate in an activity; the pursuits of an amateur are not spectator sports. Both use common tools and materials, work hard, and try to do their best to improve. You need to have both the amateur's imagination to experiment with stir-frying grapefruit and the professional's experience not to try it again.

Would it enrich our lives to pursue both approaches simultaneously rather than viewing the professional and the amateur as polar opposites?

The title of my remarks is purposely reminiscent of Isaiah Berlin's famous essay in which he distinguishes between the single-minded hedgehog (who knows one thing) and the crafty fox (who know many things).[4] This is a classic philosophical debate that places ideas into neat oppositions. In a business context, however, wouldn't it make sense for companies to have access to both the hedgehog's and the fox's perspectives depending upon the competitive landscape?

Similarly, and at a personal level, rather than pitting the professional against the amateur, wouldn't it also make sense to have access to both? Charles Ives did not abandon his passion for music when he committed himself to business. Nor did he sacrifice performance within these two arenas. His vision was simply too large on the musical front for him to be only a church organist and choir director. He was too ambitious in business to just get a job; rather, he and his partner set in place one of the first professionally run insurance agencies in the industry. Ives fit everything in and played both roles to the hilt. And he was innovative in both.

There is a second question that sometimes keeps me awake at night and that is: Would our professional roles be strengthened if we brought the amateur's approach into our work?

Again, I'll invoke the name of Charles Ives. He was well trained musically, first by his father and then as a student at Yale. He performed as a professional early in his life. But in his role as a composer, Ives displayed many of the qualities of an amateur: constant tinkering, dabbling in many different musical styles, and being open to everyday music that came from marching bands, church anthems, revival meetings—even from the dance hall. At a time when serious composers believed that there was no indigenous American music worthy of the name, Charles Ives had no embarrassment over titling a string quartet "From the Salvation Army," even though his teacher at Yale was appalled. He loved the energy and genuineness of amateurs making music just for the love of it.

Not surprisingly, Ives was given the derogatory label of "amateur" by the music establishment. The word *awful* was frequently used. Much of his musical output made no sense to listeners as he experimented with compositional ideas that had never before been heard. In fact, it wasn't until four or five decades after writing his most creative compositions that a wider public first heard his music and changed its assessment of the man from "crazy" to "genius."

A downside of professionalism can be a narrowness of perspective and a prejudice against points of view that have not been officially sanctioned. There is much to be said for pursuing paths from time to time without any concern for what others think. Our roles as professionals benefit, I believe, by welcoming on stage our "two-year-old selves"—that part of us which can poke at things without worrying about perfection and remain open to mystery. Wallace Stevens, another businessman who became in his pastime a major American poet, expresses this idea with real insight. He writes: "It is necessary to any originality to have the courage to be an amateur."[5]

Create a large enough stage for yourself to support both your professional and your amateur. Happiness surely increases from active participation in many communities, and besides, you can never be entirely certain ex-ante the source of your legacy.

Welcome your amateur on stage in your role as a professional. It takes courage to work against the grain and be authentic as amateurs are wont to do. Yet it is from authenticity that real competitive advantage may emerge and from where you have the best shot of evolving from a business professional into a truly unique artist in business.

Notes

[1] Andrew Abbott, *The System of Professions: An Essay on the Division of Expert Labor* (Chicago: University of Chicago Press, 1988).

[2] G. K. Chesterton, *All Is Grist: A Book of Essays* (New York: Dodd Mead, 1932).

[3] Wayne Booth, *For the Love of It: Amateuring and Its Rivals* (Chicago: University of Chicago Press, 1999).

[4] Isaiah Berlin, *The Hedgehog and the Fox: An Essay on Tolstoy's View of History* (London: Weidenfeld and Nicolson, 1953).

[5] Wallace Stevens, *Letters of Wallace Stevens* (Berkeley: University of California Press, 1966).

·6·

Being Silly, Seriously

Examining empirical evidence is one hallmark of the University of Chicago style, and I've learned over the years that when I am the evidence it can even be a wonderful cover for talking about myself.

In that spirit, then, I'd like to share some data about my decision to interview here for a faculty position in the early sixties. It would be tempting, of course, to tell a story that emphasized a carefully thought-out decision on my part. But to be perfectly honest, I wanted to interview here because the comedy team of Mike Nichols and Elaine May was associated in my mind with the University of Chicago. As a doctoral student at that other business school north of here, I remember listening to recordings of their funny, intellectually playful improvisations, for example, a conversation between a patient with serious psychological problems and her

Convocation Address, 481st Convocation, University of Chicago, June 12, 2005.

therapist who continues to hiccup throughout the session. Back then, I thought that an institution that would welcome people as talented and wonderfully wacky as these two must indeed be something special. All in all, it was a silly reason for selecting Chicago as a good place for a job interview.

Now I do take some comfort in the fact that others have decided to become a part of this institution for reasons that seem equally dubious. For example, the late Katharine Graham, who was publisher of the *Washington Post* and a trustee of this university, wrote about her decision to attend Chicago in her autobiography. Her father had vetoed her desire to study in London, but he told her that she could leave Vassar after her sophomore year and enroll at any college within the United States. One day while flipping through the pages of *Redbook* magazine she happened to see a picture of the handsome, newly appointed, twenty-nine-year-old president of the University of Chicago—Robert Maynard Hutchins. Not only was he good-looking, but the university was coeducational and located in a big city. In what has to be another silly reason for choosing this university, she decided to enroll.

I think some of our mentors must have been dismayed at how Graham and I took such a serious step for such silly reasons, but the outcome of our decisions did stand the ultimate empirical test: it worked. So with that as a recommendation, let me devote a few moments to the subject of being silly—sometimes.

When the word *silly* is attached to someone or to an idea, it's generally not meant as a compliment. Silly is synonymous with unsophisticated, ignorant, or lacking in common sense. Accordingly, William Frederick, Duke of Gloucester, and William IV both received the nickname "Silly Billy" to capture their foolish, empty-headed ways. We're supposed to outgrow silliness. ("Quit being so silly." "Ask a silly question, get a silly answer.")

So why would someone choose to anchor remarks on a word that many adults want to expunge rather than embrace? Is it perhaps that he has nothing serious to say? Or, could it be that he's concerned that voices within each one of us, as well as those from others, block certain apertures into serious ideas—or an aperture into serious business?

Deliberate silliness is paradoxical because it puts us in control: when we are silly, we can view the world through different lenses of our own choosing. Silliness frees the imagination, allowing us to see possibilities not constrained by the need to please someone or get everything right to pass someone else's standardized test. Being silly can mean testing the view on our own terms, trying a zoom lens, or a fish-eye lens, or a panoramic lens.

The imaginative lens stands in sharp contrast with a technical perspective, which values objectivity, neutrality, and impersonal ways of perceiving. The American poet Wallace Stevens contrasts these two lenses in his poem "Six Significant Landscapes." In the last stanza he writes:

Rationalists, wearing square hats,
Think, in square rooms,
Looking at the floor,
Looking at the ceiling,
They confine themselves
To right-angled triangles.
If they tried rhomboids,
Cones, waving ellipses—
As, for example, the ellipse of the half moon—
Rationalists would wear sombreros.

Stevens begins his poem in a linear world defined by walls, ceiling, and floor, creating a sense of being confined. And then there is a transformation into new shapes: the half moon, a sombrero, square hats put aside. It's as if he recognized that while a fish-eye lens, for instance, would ruin a passport photo, it might very well do something artful.

Indeed, being silly can be like posing before fun-house mirrors to view ourselves in multiple ways. In their silly ways, children delight in make believe, in playing "let's pretend." On any given day when I was young, I could be a magician, then a pirate, and then Superman (that is, until gravity took hold).

Regrettably, we are probably past the days of "let's pretend." But rather than searching for that one identity, in shaping our careers we can benefit from multiple identities, some of them as young as childhood, and only one as old as today.

The quintessential self-made businessman Benjamin Franklin was considerably larger than this single identity. His multiple personae, in fact, are the embodiment of a trickster—that figure in society that rattles the cage in order to challenge cultural conventions. Franklin entered the public stage at sixteen, writing as an elderly woman criticizing the hypocrisy of the elite in Massachusetts. He wrote in London newspapers sometimes as a Briton (a London manufacturer) and at other times as a New Englander (an American). He knew precisely which identity to bring on stage to reach his intended audience.

I tend to agree with the Chicago Symphony's Daniel Barenboim, who has suggested that having multiple identities is not only possible but, indeed, something to which to aspire.

If these small, but powerful, voices within each of us don't kill the imagination, the words of others can. Ideas are sometimes put down not because they are really foolish but rather because they threaten widely held beliefs.

In other cases, the put-downs have more to do with the messenger. The social psychologist Dan Wegner divides the world into two types of people: the bumblers who enjoy going through life trying to get something done and the pointers who never do anything themselves but love to point out the bumblers' bumbles. The word *silly* is a favorite weapon in the pointer's vocabulary.

Now I have to acknowledge that many, if not most, ideas labeled "silly" are just that—silly. But a small number of ideas judged to be foolish do mature and do impact the world—FedEx, eBay, even Silly Putty. Low-probability outcomes such as these pose a dilemma for organizations because a large number of tries must take place, most of which will be unsuccessful and deemed, after the fact, to have been bad investments. (It's a dilemma reminiscent of a long-standing belief in business that about half of what is spent on advertising is wasted, the only problem being that we don't know which half.)

Not unlike businesses, but in a more permissive economy, the best universities are places that tolerate, even encourage, serious dialogue about ideas that many would consider silly or foolish—perhaps even dangerous. Stuart Tave, now professor emeritus of English at this university, once opined that more dumb things happen at a university than at any other accredited institution. In a 1989 convocation address, Tave described the best faculty and students as smart, self-confident people—even a bit arrogant—who take big risks that stretch themselves to the edge and beyond, much like great athletes. And it's because of this quality of mind that they are also capable of pulling their intellectual hamstrings, making big mistakes and fools of themselves. The University of Chicago has a particular place in its heart for those who seriously pursue risky ideas. Two examples on the research front immediately come to mind.

The late Professor Subrahmanyan Chandrasekhar, who won the Nobel Prize in 1983, was severely criticized by then leading astronomer Sir Arthur Eddington for his work on the evolution of stars. Eddington tore into Chandrasekhar's work—a reductio ad absurdum, he called it—and then pronounced that there should be a "law of nature to prevent a star from behaving in this absurd way." The audience laughed. Eventually what was labeled absurd would be vindicated; his insight had been correct, and black holes would be accepted.

In the Graduate School of Business, George Stigler used to tell the story of Ronald Coase's first visit to the university, to discuss his proposition that when there are no transaction costs, the assignment of legal rights has no effect on the way economic resources would be used. Stigler wondered how such a fine economist could make such an obvious mistake. So, believing that the idea was silly enough to debate, twenty Chicago economists met with Coase. Stigler described the two-hour discussion as exhilarating, with the vote going from twenty to one against Coase at the beginning to twenty-one for Coase at the end. Ronald Coase received the Nobel Prize in 1991.

The audacious founder of this university, William Rainey Harper, crafted a vision of a great research university built in a swamp on the Midway, freed faculty to do research, doubled the top salary scale, admitted women and Jews, initiated the quarter system, and created high-quality extension programs outside of Hyde Park. Some labeled the university a veritable monstrosity: "A foreign intrusion into the life of the city." "Harper's folly." Despite the ridicule, this institution surely benefited from entertaining what some "pointers" thought was a silly, fantastic notion.

Now, some final thoughts for *your* bottom line:

First, don't take things and yourself too seriously. Keep in mind William James's counsel: "Our errors are surely not such awfully solemn things. In a world where we are so certain to incur them in spite of all our caution, a certain lightness of heart seems healthier than this excessive nervousness on their behalf."[1]

Second, engage in some actions that others may find silly. Take a train across this great country—you'll see things that you would never see from an airplane or the interstate. Accept a cut in pay to do work you love. Stroll across the monumental Brooklyn Bridge.

Third, surprise yourself and others by doing something silly every day. Tackle some project with the goal of being inefficient. Argue a side of an issue that's opposed to what you believe. Plan to be spontaneous tomorrow.

Focus your zoom lens on my silly reason for interviewing here and how it turned out to be an aperture into a life's work more satisfying than I ever could have imagined. I know that Katharine Graham had the same sense of fulfillment in the College.

Note

William James, *The Will to Believe and Other Essays in Popular Philosophy* (New York: Dover, 1956; original work published 1897).

Why Are You Here and Not Somewhere Else

Speeches by faculty members on the day of convocation at this university have a long tradition of being one last opportunity to deliver a serious lecture within a tight, twelve-minute time frame.

But wait! We're off campus this evening. I don't feel any real pressure to use terms such as *beta*, *residuals*, or *diminishing returns*. And I can talk for less or even more than twelve minutes without getting into trouble!

That being said, the stimulus for my remarks draws from the world of the arts. This is a source that might seem at first blush more relevant to a group about to receive a master of fine arts than a degree in business. But my theme this evening is not about the importance of bringing financial and intellectual capital from business to support the arts. What I do want to explore moves in just the opposite direction,

Faculty address given to graduates of the Booth School of Business, University of Chicago, June 12, 2010.

namely, what the fine arts, like painting, sculpture, music, and creative writing, can contribute to practicing the art of hands-on business leadership.

Let me begin by recalling the famous speech given by the novelist William Faulkner when he accepted the Nobel Prize for Literature in 1950. "It is [the poet's] privilege," he said, "to help man endure by lifting his heart, by reminding him of the courage and honor and hope and pride and compassion and pity and sacrifice which have been the glory of his past. The poet's voice need not merely be the record of man, it can be one of the props, the pillars to help him endure and prevail."[1]

I think we would all agree that there's an important place for intangible values in a world that sometimes relies too heavily on material facts and the belief that if something can't be measured, then it isn't real. The artist shows us what values may be missing.

Beyond values, however, there are other artistic qualities worth considering in a business context. For example:

- The artist explores connotative meanings— the hidden, emotional, indefinable aspects of things.
- Artists are often change agents who push against rules, convey messages that otherwise would go unheard, and force us to think differently about others and about ourselves.

- The artist relishes paradox and ambiguity
  and accepts that problems often have more than
  one solution, that questions have more than one
  answer.

We don't need to look very far to illustrate these artistic qualities. As many of you know, the Harper Center is now home to a significant art collection selected by a committee chaired by my colleague, Professor Canice Prendergast.

The works displayed throughout the building raise interesting issues for the viewer, for example, biases in an outsider's perception of events, the fading of memory, the chilling effect of censorship, the fine line between banality and beauty, and taking on challenges. I find myself captivated by an installation on the third floor titled *The Russian Ending*. This group of twenty images shows how Danish filmmakers in the 1920s would alter the endings of films for American versus Russian audiences, all of the Russian movies ending in calamity while the American endings show everyone living happily ever after. Cultures do differ—a useful perspective to hold in this global economy.

On the way to teach my business policy class early in the winter quarter, I noticed a new sculpture near one of the main stairways. Made of white neon, it contained eight words.

My first thought was, Why is this sculpture located along a stairway? I observed that most students and faculty heading to or from class didn't even seem to notice it. Was the artist reminding us that in pursuing a destination, we often pay little attention to things along the way?

I then speculated that maybe it was located in the business school because neon has a long association with the field of marketing—you have seen the signs for "No Vacancy" or "Hot Food and Cold Beer."

But these words were quite different. They read:

WHY ARE YOU HERE AND NOT SOMEWHERE ELSE

The creator of this sculpture, Danish artist Jeppe Hein, states that his art isn't anything on its own but only what the public informs it with, that is, what the public brings to the experience of engaging with his art.

Well, this professor has been informing Hein's work regularly since it was installed. And for me, the words hold useful ideas in thinking about the pre-work required for practicing the art of effective leadership.

To illustrate, let me repeat these words with different emphases:

WHY ARE YOU HERE AND NOT SOMEWHERE ELSE

The word *here* points to context, the ability to read a situation, to be street smart, if you will. As a leader, what's important for me to know about the history and culture of an organization? What issues are ripe for people within this organization? Who are key opinion leaders and where are the critics and naysayers?

In my experience, leaders can sometimes skim over the "here." It's tempting to assume that one's success in a prior context will simply transfer to another or to take the preemptive position that "*I'm* here to make decisions, not to waste time listening." Acknowledging the "here" requires being fully present to one's surroundings. It requires the ability to describe what one sees without immediately interpreting it, and it takes a lot of patience.

Or how about this emphasis: "

WHY ARE YOU HERE AND NOT SOMEWHERE ELSE

The word *why* identifies the issue around which a leader wants others to engage. The issue and how it's communicated is really critical in attracting and inspiring others to follow.

One can find many compelling examples of leaders who are clear about the issue. Consider Lou Gerstner's first meeting with the fifty top people at IBM. Brought in as CEO from the outside in 1993 to deal with the company's enormous challenges at that time, he cut right to the chase in defining three issues at that very first meeting: eliminate bureaucracy, downsize rapidly, and offer customers comprehensive solutions.

The "why" word is sometimes elusive. A leader may focus on too many issues, which only serves to generate confusion or dissipate energy. He or she sometimes gets tired or bored with a core issue and ends up introducing a stream of issues du jour. Or a leader may engage with an audience that walks away from a meeting (or a speech, dare I say) wondering if there was any "why" at all. There is no substitute for a convincing, recognizable "why."

Looking up at the white neon sculpture from that stairway, I focused in on another word:

WHY ARE YOU HERE AND NOT SOMEWHERE ELSE

Emphasizing the "you" forces me to consider what personal qualities I could use to make progress on some important issue in a particular context. It's common, I suppose, to believe that leaders who succeed during times of great challenge are somehow bigger than life in the Thomas Carlyle sense from *On Heroes, Hero-Worship, and the Heroic in History*. But a strong case can be made that those who accomplish great things are not dramatically different from many of the people sitting in this audience.

Historians have pointed out that Winston Churchill did not have great success in his career either before or following the Second World War. Yet, in the early stages of that war, when England was desperate for a voice of supreme courage, Churchill gave the nation exactly that. What had been his weaknesses, and would later return as such, were, during that brief period, great strengths.

Katharine Graham never anticipated becoming publisher of the *Washington Post*. Yet, following her husband's tragic suicide, she became the only credible bridge between her father, who had purchased the paper, and her son who eventually took over. And despite an initial lack of confidence, she ended up playing that bridging role brilliantly.

The "you" requires self-awareness to play one's role authentically. But it also requires insight and the courage to step away when changes in the context or the issues no longer fit the authentic "you."

And then there's that final phrase in Hein's sculpture:
WHY ARE YOU HERE, AND NOT SOMEWHERE ELSE

So many "somewheres" to consider these days . . . Should I commit to one of the conventional paths in business? What about my passion for building something from scratch or joining others who are? Should I use my education in other domains such as education or public service?

Having abundant choices is certainly good news. You have an opportunity to choose the right stage on which to perform and to do that repeatedly throughout your career. And I know that many of you are engaged in doing just that. Yet, I would also warn that a downside to all of the possibilities presented by these other "somewheres" might be a lessened commitment to the stage that you are on now. Leaders must find something about the "here" that they care about in order to sustain commitment.

Allow me to share a personal note. I haven't paid much attention to the "somewhere else," not because I have tenure, as you might hypothesize, but because I love this university, its history, its values, and most important its people—faculty, students, and staff.

The artist Jeppe Hein was probably surprised that his sculpture ended up in a business school, let alone to learn now that it served as a stimulus for my remarks this evening. But his provocative creation reminds those of us deeply interested in business that beyond the analytic mode of thinking, there is another mode of thinking that is complementary and, I would assert, essential for the practice of leadership. This, the artistic mode, goes deeper.

One final observation: our Danish artist leaves us with more ambiguity. There is no question mark (or even a period) at the end of eight words. Is he being playful, I wondered, adding uncertainty, or did he simply run out of money or glass?

Perhaps his sculpture was not intended as a question at all, but rather, as an invitation to rearrange these words as a declarative sentence that reads: "I am here, and not somewhere else, because . . ."

I rather like that rephrasing. It's intentional and practical. It focuses a leader's day-to-day actions in confronting the large strategic decisions. And a declarative sentence like that also guides one in dealing with the myriad of small, tactical, and people-related decisions that will largely determine whether *any* strategy gets implemented effectively.

Perhaps most important, however, is the value of knowing why I am here and not somewhere else as it relates to the personal side of the ledger. As such, this knowledge clarifies and enhances our roles as members of families, local organizations, and communities—and even in our capacities as national and global citizens.

Note

[1] William Faulkner, *Essays, Speeches, and Public Letters,* ed. James B. Meriwether (New York: Random House, 1965), 120.